To my smart and silly nephew Bray Bray, don't ever forget you're a king..
-A.M.M.

To mi ahijada preciosa, you will be great and make a difference in the world.
-J.W.

That's My Baby!
Text copyright © 2018 Ashley Maxie-Moreman
Illustrations copyright © 2018 Joanah Whitely
ISBN-13: 978-0-6920790-6-5

All rights reserved. This book may not be reproduced in whole or in part in any form, or by any means, without express written permission from the publisher.

Adventures of Bray Bray, LLC.
5927 SW 70th St. South Miami, FL 33243
AdventuresofBrayBray.com

That's My Baby!

written by Ashley Maxie-Moreman

illustrated by Joanah Whitely

Wow sweetie!
Look how your toes wiggle.

Oh, honey!
Look how your legs squiggle.

Aww baby!
Look how your arms squeeze.

Yay genius!
Look how you write your ABC's.

Oh, my goodness!
Look how your hair grows.

What a cutie!
Look how your skin glows.

That's my baby!
Look how you smile so brightly,
While I hold you in my arms
so tightly.

CPSIA information can be obtained
at www.ICGtesting.com
Printed in the USA
BVHW011246100323
660185BV00003BA/6